POWER HO'OPONOPONO

www.christine-salopek.de
info@christine-salopek.de

Original edition:
Christine & Robert Salopek
Power Ho'oponopono
Published in Germany by:
Lüchow in J. Kamphausen Mediengruppe GmbH, Bielefeld 2013

The Images for the cover are from:
Wilfried Klei (ocean), stock photo 551583_Cliff Daley (a happy dolphin),
Fotolia_Subbotina Anna (flowers),
Dolphin icon: Wilfried Klei from fotolia_jwm

Christine und Robert Salopek –
Power Ho'oponopono
© tao.de in J. Kamphausen
Mediengruppe GmbH, Bielefeld 2014
info@tao.de

Proofreading: Annabelle Mayntz
Reviewed by: Lindy McMullin
Cover design:
Kristina Hoehn/Wilfried Klei
Layout and typesetting: Wilfried Klei

www.tao.de

1st edition 2014

Bibliographic information published by the Deutsche Nationalbibliothek
The German National Library lists this publication in the Deutsche Nationalbibliografie;
detailed bibliographic data are available under the following internet address:
http://dnb.d-nb.de.

ISBN Print Edition: 978-3-95529-190-7

Christine & Robert Salopek

POWER HO'O PONOPONO

Translation into English
by Vidya Marina Bolz

tao.de

The philosophy of Ho'oponopono

'Heal yourself and thus heal the world'-

or as the Chinese saying goes:

'If everybody swept in front of their own door,

the entire world would be clean.'

Christine Salopek:

'Ho'oponopono – when I read this word for the first time I could not even pronounce it correctly. It took me weeks until I could say it properly. Today it is quite natural and internalized in my heart. It has changed our lives.'

Table of Contents:

Foreword

In Europe the following four key phrases are known and applied in regard to the Ho'oponopono principle:

I am sorry.

I forgive myself.

Thank you.

I love you.

However, by now we know the principle of the Hawaiian Ho'oponopono is actually a family tradition, which is passed on from generation to generation. On the various islands and also in the individual families we find dramatically different forms of this principle, as personalized and change different to unique as one finds in our individual characteristics as human beings. In some families for example the emphasis is only on 'Pono'. Each family has created the principle over the years according to their individual taste. It is very much comparable to our family tradition of potato salad recipes. Each family has its own recipe, sometimes with vinegar and oil, sometimes with mayonnaise, sometimes with broth. For some people one absolutely has to add onions, for others cucumbers are a must; for some pickled gherkins, for others salad cucumbers. There are recipes for cold or warm potato salads, and each generation alters the recipe according to their tastes, for example, with or without bacon. However, the foundation and root of the recipe always remains the same: *potatoes*

In a similar fashion, one can find the various Ho'oponopono traditions of individual families who not that in many instances have been active and lived with their traditions for many years; as different as they may appear to be in form, they all have the same common ground.

Each person takes FULL responsibility for his/her life.

Only through its usage in the West and especially in European countries, has Ho'oponopono now become very distinctly structured, which is how most people know and apply it. In this book we'd like to introduce the extended development of Ho'oponopono to Power Ho'oponopono, which then actually comes closer to its original principle. What exactly is meant by this, shall be explained later.

Taking into account the example of potato salad and the Hawaiian Tradition, we would like to invite you to eventually develop and create your very own Ho'oponopono, that would appeal to your very own personal tastes and suit you. In this way it returns to the free principle, which in reality it is, as it has always been.

Introduction

Now here is the true story of how the principle of Ho'oponopono became known in Europe....

For those of you reading it for the first time today, we can only say: we were so touched by this story years ago we immediately started applying the principle, to experience ourselves, what was possible.

We had heard a story about a therapist in Hawaii, who had healed an entire infirmary ward full of criminal, mentally ill patients – without ever having met a single one of them in person. It was said that the psychologist had studied the files of the occupants and had then had directed his attention within himself to find out how he had created the diseases of these people. As he worked on himself the condition of each of the occupants also improved. It was said the therapist replace was using with used the Hawaiian principle called Ho'oponopono.

As already mentioned above:

> *'Heal yourself and thus heal the world.' Or as the Chinese saying goes: 'If everybody swept in front of their door, the entire world would be clean'*

The fundamental assumption of this principle is that everybody is fully responsible for everything that appears in his/her life or in his/her field of reality – circumstances, people, diseases etc.

At the very beginning of our journey we had always understood the phrase 'to take full responsibility', to mean we are fully responsible for what we think and do. Everything else is not within the bounds of our responsibility.

After all the experiences and talks that we have had in the last few years regarding Ho'oponopono most people understand it in a similar fashion. It is quite alright and accepted one is responsible for something one personally does or does not do. What somebody else does, however, is none of our business; we are not responsible for it.

This is exactly where the mistake is, because this is not true!

You can find a detailed explanation for this in Chapter 1, which takes a closer look at the topic 'vibration and resonance'.

Let's go back to the Hawaiian therapist. His name is Dr. Ihaleakala Hew Len. He taught a new perspective to us, of 'taking full responsibility' thus enabling him to heal all the psychologically imbalanced people in the hospital ward mentioned earlier.

Dr. Len never saw a single patient whom he was treating face to face. He simply read the files on his desk. While he was reading the files he worked on himself internally. While he worked on himself the healing of the patient began. After a few months the patients who normally had to be locked up were allowed to move around freely. Others who were heavily medicated could be taken off the medications. And those who had no chance of ever being released were allowed to go free. Today that entire hospital unit is closed due to lack of patients.

What did Dr. Len do to make this possible? He simply healed that part of himself within, presented to him on the outside, as a mirror image, in the form of a patient.

Dr. Len explained that 'assuming full responsibility' means that everything that appears in your life – simply BECAUSE it is in your life – is your responsibility.

Dr. Len was asked how he healed himself. What did he do exactly while he looked at the files of the patients?

He replied: "I simply kept repeating:

> *'I am sorry' and 'I love you'"*.
>
> (Vitale, Joe and Len, Ihaleakala Hew, Zero Limits, see bibliography.)

Here again are the core phrases of Ho'oponopono, as they are known and used in European countries:

I am sorry.

I forgive myself.

Thank you.

I love you.

With this principle of Ho'oponopono, which is amplified through Christine's symbols, we have achieved fabulous successes ourselves. However, at some point, this way of phrasing did not feel right for us, any more.

If my action is authentic and comes from the heart, I do not have to feel sorry for it. I am prepared to take responsibility for it, but NOT take on suffering.

At this point, like so many other times in our work, we felt a new path had to be explored. This is the path we would like to take you on: a path more authentic and powerful for us, than the phrases that have been used so far.

This is the path from the Ho'oponopono principle to the **POWER HO'OPONOPONO** principle!

This book is about the realization that the original principle needs to be adjusted to the NEW ERA; and this new principle in its NEWNESS as well, comes closer to the original legacy of the indigenous people of Hawaii.

How did we come to this realization?

After having practiced the ....principle extensively in our lives for almost two years, – always involving, however, the symbols of Archangel Michael and Archangel Chamuel, which Christine received from the Angels specifically for that purpose – at some point we had to stop using it, in spite of all our good experiences and the changes, which had been exceptionally wonderful. The application of the symbols had especially contributed an immediate acceleration and tremendous energy boost to the entire principle.

We could no longer use it in its original phraseology nor teach it in our seminars in this form any longer.

Something was no longer authentic. However, for quite some time we did not know what it was. *I am sorry.... I am sorry... I am sorry...*, we could just not say these words any longer.

But why not? It had worked really well up to this point.

We had learned to allow situations and resistance to come up without warning on our path; to be present without wanting to change things or judge them. This is how we handled the situation, by accepting it was the way it was.

One day we went for a walk and suddenly received a spark of inspiration to replace, 'I am sorry' with the following words:

"I take full responsibility for my actions, for everything that I have done or not done."

'I forgive myself' was replaced by the following words:

"And I am at peace with it."

These phrases felt very good and authentic to us.

We both felt continuous chills. What do we mean by this? It was like having a goosebumps shower repeatedly across our arms and over our entire body.

Some time passed and then we had the confirmation from the outside as a clear and simple clue for us: 'DO IT!' Bring this innovation amongst the people and trust your perceptions.' Not that we did not trust our perceptions, but at first we kept these changes private amongst ourselves and used them only for ourselves.

Why come up with this book now?

Based on our own experiences with this new principle, which we now call Power Ho'oponopono, as well as in our experiences in the seminars and feedback from them, this principle wants to come out into the world and be shared now.

We received additional confirmation via a woman, a seminar participant, who had lived in Hawaii for a long time and who brought us into contact with a man from Hawaii.

He could only shake his head regarding the traditional phrases that have been so far in Europe and he explained:

Why should he ask for pardon and forgiveness when all he did was act authentically from the heart; he was in perfection as perfectly as he could be, at that particular moment of his existence?

This attitude results from the fact Hawaiians have been brought up with this principle and so have integrated it, living in full acceptance of everything in the NOW. For generations, families have passed the information down individually.

It is fascinating this principle is used and implemented in Hawaii even in the courts, public offices, municipal authorities, simply in every possible conflict, as well as in daily life and within families.

In addition to this, we have recently heard that in the United States, the principle of Ho'oponopono is an APPROVED TREATMENT METHOD! Incredible!

We want to bring this work back as a totally individual and free principle. in a manner corresponding more closely to the original Hawaiian principle, and we would like to make it possible for each person to develop his/her own tradition, to implement it for himself/herself and to be able to pass it on.

We support and reinforce this principle through the power of the symbols are enclosed at the end of this book.

Chapter 1

The Power Ho'oponopono Principle

For us it is one of the most sensational methods you can use to help yourself lead a harmonious, happy existence, in every single area of your life!

Is it possible!

We have experienced ourselves, how the effect of Power Ho'oponopono takes effect, and how magnificent the changes are, that have happened in our life and can happen ion yours too. In the areas of health, relationship, family, occupation and finances. The principle and its effects have been very much intensified for us through the additional application of the symbols. However, please simply try it out and feel it for yourself.

Everything we are talking and writing about here, we have internalized ourselves and we live with these insights. Due to this, in discordant situations, we still ask ourselves the one and ONLY question:

'What does this have to do with ME?'

This is the foundation upon which the principle is based. After all, you are responsible for EVERYTHING in your life. Are you now ready to be fully responsible for everything in your life?

This is the prerequisite that enables the Power Ho'oponopono principle to take effect.

And we really mean EVERYTHING.

Not only for what is being spoken or thought but also really for simply EVERYTHING that occurs in your life and in your reality. Everything you are, that you feel or think, and everything deposited and stored in your energy body creates resonance. Let us have a look at a few basic topics and the kind of questions we encounter in our daily life.

- Why do I always end up with the same type of man or woman?
- Why do I always have this reoccurring situation in my life?
- Why do I always end up at the same point?
- Why do I always lack money?

- Why do I feel lack of affection, of love or also lack in other areas of my life?

The list of these sorts of questions could just go on and on.

Many people become concerned with this kind of inquiry only when they find themselves in a hopeless situation, and then possibly ask 'Why?' and 'What does this have to do with me?' Perhaps you are familiar with such a situation, in which prayer often seems to be the last resort. At this point we would then ask ourselves why should one even find oneself in such an extreme situation. Rather, one can consciously look at oneself, at one's life and those kinds of situations, before it even gets there.

The fact you have to take full responsibility for everything in your life, is exactly how it is! This is part of the natural law of vibration. These natural laws are functioning whether we want it, believe in it, act and live according to it or not. They ALWAYS work as these are the Laws of Nature.

Everybody is familiar to some extent with at least some sayings in regard to the natural law of vibration, or in fact might have even vocalized some of them.

- *Like attracts like.*
- *The outer is the reflection of the inner.*
- *Show me your friends and I'll tell you, who YOU are.*

- *As within, so without.*
- *Whatever one shouts into the woods, that is what will echo back.*

All of this has to do with the natural law of vibration. However, for a long time we have not been aware of the implications of this wisdom: which is so much more extensive than we can possibly grasp with our minds. This insight has even been scientifically verified:

We take in 70 million kilobits of information in with our senses per second. Our mind processes some 72 kilobits of this per second, which corresponds to 9 conscious perceptions per second, leaving us with some 5 perceptions per second. This roughly corresponds to a ping-pong ball (our mind) on a football field (our energy body). Now try to imagine how much information is available; how much vibration and energy is not perceived by the mind, the ping-pong ball, what is excluded and what is not perceived or even recognized. The vibrations from the football field are also 'shouted out into the woods' so to speak, so one must take responsibility for this entire area that is unobservable and not only that which is consciously sent out from the mind.

THEREFORE: There is so much more that affects us in our resonance/vibration than we think or consciously perceive and live.

And it is now a matter of taking full responsibility for everything that vibrates on the conscious level (ping-pong ball) on the unconscious level (football field). Your day-to-day life is therefore the projection of your entire vibration.

Only when you discover this and accept it, do you have the possibility to make sustainable changes in your life.

Only one change on the conscious level, (ping-pong ball) for example through positive thinking, will not produce a permanent change in the unconscious (football field).

The ping-pong ball will never be able to change the vibration of the football field permanently.

Everything in your life appears as a mirror image, as a guide for your life.

Using another example, we would like to illustrate why it is so and what fantastic opportunities arise out of it, so you can take your life in your own hands.

When I get up in the morning and stand in front of the mirror in the bathroom, I notice I look somewhat crumpled, that I am not shaven, that my hair is all over the place, and that I have circles under my eyes. I can look in the mirror and say: 'You look really lousy today.' I can then drape a towel over the mirror because I don't want to look at that miserable condition any longer. However, I am out of luck, because on my way to the kitchen I pass by another mirror in the hallway and again see the same crumpled image as a reflection. Now the best move would be to drape that mirror as well, to avoid being confronted with it again. An alternative would be to change something right in the bathroom in front of the first mirror.

But now let's be totally honest:

Who would get the idea to spread the shaving cream or make-up with relish onto the mirror directly, in order to shave the mirror or to make it more beautiful? Everybody shaves his OWN face or applies make-up on her OWN face, and then knows that he/she looks good again and that it feels good and refreshing that way. Well, unfortunately the reality in day-to-day life looks totally different. With shaving or applying make-up it is obvious to you that it is pointless trying to achieve change in the mirror image. Nobody would attempt that. Everybody would think that totally ridiculous. In daily life, however, everybody is very quick to assign things to the other (=mirror image) and to find fault or mistake in the other. Doing that is easy, and one does not have to look at one's own self. But also in life the outside is just the mirror image.

Now, how was it again with shaving?

There is the neighbor with his obstinate attitude who is to blame that one now even has to go to court. One really has no other choice. There is the preposterous boss, the dim-witted work colleague and all the others to blame that you are bullied or that work is not enjoyable any more. The partner has preferably to change first, of course. He/she, of course has to take you as you are. Yes, nothing whatsoever has to be changed on your side because you are not responsible, it's always others who are to blame and who are responsible. With all these examples we want to show you how the law of resonance works.

However, it is also true you don't trigger some situations consciously, because you have not decided in your mind (on the conscious level) to send out these vibrations. And yet you are responsible for it because you have triggered it with your vibration from your football field and thus you caused it and have to be responsible for it. For the vibration it does not make any difference whether you have sent it out consciously or unconsciously. The vibration is simply energy, following the law of resonance.

As in the bathroom, you can only change your mirror image by shaving YOURSELF or applying make-up on YOURSELF, in other words, by changing your energy, by removing disturbing patterns, by harmonizing. Not just on the level of the ping-pong ball, but on the entire football field. In order to achieve a causal improvement and change it is not enough to merely think positively for a period of a few days or weeks.

To reflect about something and then want to change it with strategy, tactic or with calculation is not going to produce anything, because the ping-pong ball (the mind) will NEVER be able to re-direct your football field into a different vibration, at least not permanently and sustainably. This is why positive thinking does not work. Certainly one can force something momentarily with the mind, but it will cost effort and energy as it goes against the vibration of the football field.

Only if this happens in harmony with your football field, from the heart, will change be visible also in your environment. Only that which is felt in the heart and which is changed from the heart can bring about a causal and permanent change.

You'll find an explanation regarding the palpable difference between ego/mind and 'being in the heart'/feeling in chapter 2.

As has already been mentioned before:

'If everybody would sweep in front of their own door the entire world would be clean.'

It would be even better to sweep WITHIN your own house.

At this point we would like to emphasize two additional things:
In the first place this gives us the POWER to live consciously and renew everything within our own field of responsibility, that also changes things. You always have a choice as to what you are going to shout in the woods and through the

echo, automatically change what resounds back from the woods. This is Mandatory – it is the law!

Secondly, it is important you become aware of the following. It is possible to change everything if you are ready to change your own vibration and to accept responsibility for all your actions and non-actions. Consequently it is clear: even if you do not do something, you have made the decision NOT to DO it.

One more time: it should be remembered that ONLY your own vibration has to be changed, the mirror images, the projections on the outside, will change inevitably with it.

The unfriendly waiter, the rude neighbor, the preposterous boss, the phony girlfriend… what changes and who even leaves your field of resonance and with that leaves your vibration, your life? This not that can happen, that people simply leave, that one drifts apart, no longer attracting one another.

Now at this point, fears will rise up again. If you now feel fear of loss…that is fantastic, because you can immediately start working on this fear first. Here, TRUST is missing: in the big Oneness, trust in the guidance and trust that everything happens for your own good – and with that, trust in all the experiences that you have had so far, which make up your past. You have received this book by coincidence. It has been placed into your lap now, so you can take charge of your life in a powerful way and change it.

After a period of practice, you can apply Power Ho'oponopono, combined with the symbols at all times and everywhere in your mind: In the car, while eating, while shopping, at work, on the street or in the shower. That sounds like work! Well, it is actually, but it will attract happiness, love and much more into your life.

A few more examples:

If you feel cheated by a business partner and you know in your mind that you yourself would never cheat, the energy of deceit is nevertheless present in your energy body, in your football field, and it is thus visible on the outside as a reflection of your inner vibration.

If you have a work colleague who is a bully, it is you who is responsible for it, for the lack of respect towards you, because this energy is present somewhere in your football field, even if only somewhere at the furthest corner flag. The question you have to ask yourself is: 'Where do I have lack of respect?' Life will not always be able to reflect the situations and the pictures to you one to one.

If you have lack of funds in your account then the energy of lack is present somewhere WITHIN YOU. Now you can ask yourself what that could be: for example, lack of feeling of self-worth and continual sacrifice for the family or in your work. Or lack of trust, lack of self-love, lack of attentiveness, lack of self-esteem, lack of confidence, lack of compassion, lack of humility etc.

Find out where the lack has been lodged in you. Here you should pay full attention to which issue is not in harmony within you and in which areas of your life it manifests.

Thus lack can manifest itself in your account or in other areas. Our soul is trying to show us issues that concern us and that we are allowed to change in this life. More precisely, in that area of life in which the soul perceives the best possibility to reach us is where we are most likely to respond the earliest and the fastest and where we are ready to initialize changes.

For instance: in the case of a successful businessman, who is doing really well financially, the soul will choose health or relationships as a mirror. This is one example that we have encountered many times on our journey. So far, we have not found a really happy businessman, whose life was happy, although financially he was doing really fantastically. This does not mean there are no happy businessmen. Of course there are!

We have been able to successfully give the keys to 'Becoming Happy' to to many of them, but please remember that when you initiate change, you must do this from the heart. Only from this level can you reach the football field and only then will it change permanently.

By the way this has also been verified scientifically; to operate from the heart is so much more powerful than to act from the mind.

An American institute has demonstrated that the electrical power of the heart is 60 times stronger that that of the mind (ECG –EEG) and that the magnetic force of the heart is some 5000 times stronger than that of our mind. Once again one could say, "Wow, how much potential there is available, in us, in me and also in you! How effectively, efficiently and easily things can change if only one knew how to use the power of nature and natural laws for self preservation. Acting from the heart, from the football field, one gets into the power of fully and totally accepting responsibility for everything in one's life. Everything you are involved in, even if 'only' as an onlooker, has something to do with you and your internal self. Taking responsibility for this makes you powerful.

It is important to understand and accept you exist not only with your mind, the ping-pong ball, but with your entire soul, the football field.

If you can accept this, you have a key in hand, a key to your power. Through this awareness you are offered the opportunity to dissolve disharmony, presented to you via resonance, whilst remaining fully responsible. This is the pure power to hold life itself in your heart. Use this knowledge for yourself.

Have the courage to implement your own creativity and leave the game, in which you are 'lived' by others.

YOU live your own life, with joy and enthusiasm.

Chapter 2

The difference between Ego/ Mind and "Being in the Heart"

So far we've learned not to allow our actions to be motivated by ego and intellect, but to act from the power of the Heart.

How can you learn to do this?

By unconditionally implementing the very first feeling/ impulse, or the first gut feeling you have inside you. Every single day. It's really hard at first, but the more you practice and simply do it, the better you'll know YOU.

Now we do not claim that if you do this, the results will always be what you want them to be, or that this will always be the right thing.

It is certainly always the BEST: BEST for getting to know your inner structures and all the mechanisms within you; programs and mechanisms within you that act both positively and negatively.

Do you understand this? Insofar as you unconditionally implement the first impulse, no matter how weird, crazy or impossible you feel it to be, you will get to know your true self, and bit by bit your ego retreats into the background because it is caught – every day ANEW.

This is how we learned it – had to learn it – without having this explanation. Since our change, this opening of consciousness, or however you want to call it, we have simply always acted from that which came as an impulse, and often rather painfully learned that we have acted from our ego (especially for the first two years on this new path). At the time we were so sure our every act came from the Heart with every decision. Absolutely sure!

Today we know that this was the only way for us to experience and learn. Through every experienced situation came the insights: insights we had personally felt and experienced. Everything you feel and experience yourself is much easier to implement and pass on to other people, as compared to mere reading about it and theoretical understanding of it.

You can read 10 books about golf, but can you then say you can play golf? You can read this book about Power Ho'oponopono a dozen times but you will not experience its effects if you don't DO it, or only do it half-heartedly.

Continuous practice will deliver the fruits of this work to you served on a silver platter. You will feel the difference more and more whether you are acting from the Heart and its inner innate power or just from the mind.

Now begin to change your life, to cure and solve your life-situations using the force of Power of Ho'oponopono.

The most important thing here is: be honest with yourself, even when setbacks come up, or when the presumed Path of the Heart terminates in a dead-end. Turn around, out of the impasse and move on ...!

There comes a time when you can clearly differentiate between ego / mind and real power of the Heart guidance. At that moment, when you are truly yourself you'll see where you are. Whether in the heart or the ego. For us the change came when we realized we could truly allow people to be, despite their opinions and comments that were sometimes under the belt, because we came from Heart. Just leave them alone and observe: "What has that got to do with us"? What do we have inside us that we have attracted this or that Reaction/Action? What is it that works in us to provoke the different feelings and resistance? Feelings such as anger, hurt, feeling under attack, envy, sadness, fear, etc.

So with everything that happened we began to ask ourselves:

"What does this have to do with ME/US?"

This for us, was the beginning of the Ho'oponopono Work that grew more and more in our hearts and thus also in our lives. We began to glow from inside out. Slowly but steadily.

We will write down one thing in all the examples of the power of Ho'oponopono, something we are always happy to use at our events, because pretty much everyone there FEELS the difference between "speak from the Mind or speak from the bottom of your Heart". FEEL! FEEL IT FOR YOURSELF.

The example 'when it comes to your own children'... (explained later in the text!)

After completing these explanations we now pass over to the use of the Power Ho'oponopono with the four associated symbols. Readers who have not read our first book may be wondering "But where do these symbols come from anyway?"

Chapter 3

The Symbols

By Christine Salopek:

Shortly before my first Heart Opening seminar, the energy fields, which I had begun to see with my own eyes, were joined by the Symbols. This was about 8 months after I saw the spirals and shapes (=the energy fields) for the first time in 2006. My eyes had already become used to seeing the flying energy fields in the sky.

I can still vividly remember the first symbol I saw: I was just driving along in my car when something slightly colored flashed in the sky. First I thought it was a reflection of the sun or something similar. Then I saw it again. It was pink. I pulled over to the roadside, stopped, and looked at the sky. I knew these fields, and there was something in the middle of them that didn't belong there. I had no idea what it was. At first I didn't identify it as a symbol. I took out a pen and notepaper from the glove compartment of my car and drew what I saw. It disappeared as I finished and I've never seen it again. I received a task from my angels the very next day, to go into the forest with paper and pen.

There was a clearing in the forest where I often used to go and sit when I did not feel quite well or needed some peace. I decided to go there with my backpack and my blanket. I spread it out on the forest floor, sat down and began to pray. I did this often since my Opening. Earlier, I had never prayed and now it belonged to my daily routine. I prayed whenever it occurred to me, no matter where I was. In the car, while shopping, in Nature ... anywhere. Mostly in my own words, but very often the "Our Father".

In the forest I looked up into the sky, with pen and pad by my side and waited. I waited for the symbols, which, according to my Angel, I should record, but they did not come. I sat there for at least 2 hours, meditated a while, and began once more to doubt. I thought to myself: "Maybe I imagined this whole thing." At this time I often doubted myself, what I was doing, and simply everything. I doubted, even though I received more and more evidence from the outside. Evidence in the form of healing and that people who came to me began to see, hear and feel. In other words, they became also clairvoyant, clairaudient and / or sensitive. I saw their spirit guides and could often connect with their friends from the spirit world so as to access their heart energy and open or intensify the gifts and abilities associated with it. And nevertheless, the Path repeatedly threw me back into the depths that were within me, and the only thing that kept me going was my love for the angels, the love that so suddenly had taken possession of my heart, and above all, that I could see these formations, these symbols, in the heavens with open eyes. That always gave me the courage to go on and convinced me that I wasn't crazy. I really do see them up there....

Back to the clearing in the forest: I now just wanted to get up and pack everything away, since obviously there was nothing happening. I was often stubborn in moments in which I wanted an answer and there wasn't one – stubborn and impatient! It occurred to me later that day that I was none of these things. I took it naturally that nothing had happened, filled with the contentment and serenity I increasingly experienced in Nature and headed home. But then it happened. As soon as I had dropped the expectations, something colored flashed in the corner of my eye. I immediately took the pen and paper from my backpack, sat down and drew, one after the other, all the symbols that appeared.

I sat there like a child unwrapping gifts, it was so exciting and I had so much joy in my heart. I devoted myself to the symbols, completely in the moment. On this day eleven symbols appeared, so with the first, I now had twelve. Twelve symbols to work with in my first seminar, but I didn't have the faintest idea what they all meant. Yet this also came to me. I painted each one, looked deeply into each, and fell in love with them. I couldn't describe this feeling in any other way. We grew together, and I slowly built a close relationship with them, as if they were my own babies. Well, today I know, naturally, why I felt that way about them back then: because they are all parts of me, from my innermost depths, with which I have often worked. However, at that time I had no idea, since I developed everything step by step myself. Alone and as I was instructed by the guidance of the angels.

The meanings dawdled along slowly, but in time, and just one day before the first Heart Opening seminar, the meanings were all present. It was once again new territory for me, and my excitement was immeasurable. I was on the verge of cancelling the first seminar because of an invented illness or suchlike, but I couldn't bring myself to do it. It was during the time in which I had already moved out of my home, and I really needed the money that the participants had already sent me. Yes, you read that right – if I had had the possibility of paying back the money, I would have blown off the whole seminar. I was so terrified of my first seminar, I would have preferred to sink into the ground than do it. I had no plan, no seminar schedule, NOTHING. Only the symbols, the energy fields and me. Every time I sat down, wanting to create a seminar schedule, NOTHING came. My head was empty every time. Every time there came only this word from the world of spirit: TRUST. Hmmm …… I was stubborn, but because of my terrestrial financial situation I really had no other choice but to hold the seminar. And what can I tell you, it was incredible! After I had introduced myself to the participants the words began to gush, and amazed, I heard myself speaking as if the words belonged to someone else. Then I presented a seminar schedule that I didn't even know I had – until that very moment. All the nervousness was gone. There was only the trust that I felt.

I was so guided by the angels that the time just flew by. I received a lot of information about the participants. Things I couldn't possibly know, and suchlike. A great deal of proof for my mind, and many things occurred, which have allowed both me and of course the participants to grow. Allowed to grow in our core of divinity.

Yes, that was the beginning of the symbols that have been happening within me, and still are. One final thing I'd like to mention: I never saw a symbol twice. They appeared only until I had recorded them, and then they were gone again.

I saw a symbol externally only for as long as I needed to inwardly receive it, understand it and internally integrate it and until its energy was present within me.

You'll find the four symbols used in Power Ho'oponopono on the following pages.

1. The symbol of Archangel Michael:

For resolution, harmonization and perfect acceptance of everything that is NOW.

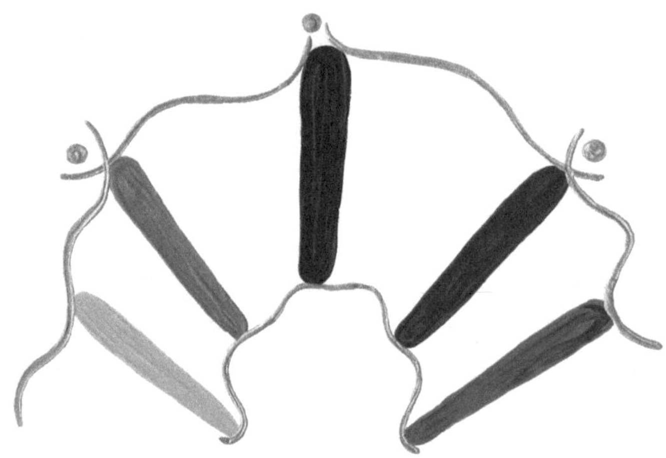

Brief description:

The five light-sabers of yellow, green, blue, purple and pink.

This symbol is to be used as a protection and to dissolve sticky energy, to separate or to harmonize. But mainly it's about accepting your own greatness and power! This symbol will help you with that task.

It's important to mention that owning a sword does not necessarily imply you must draw it in combat. I very much enjoy working with Archangel Michael and am grateful I have been shown his potentials.

Here in Power Ho'oponopono you need solely the blue sword for resolution, harmonization and the perfect acceptance of everything that is NOW.

2. *The symbol of Archangel Gabriel:*

To be in harmony and peace.

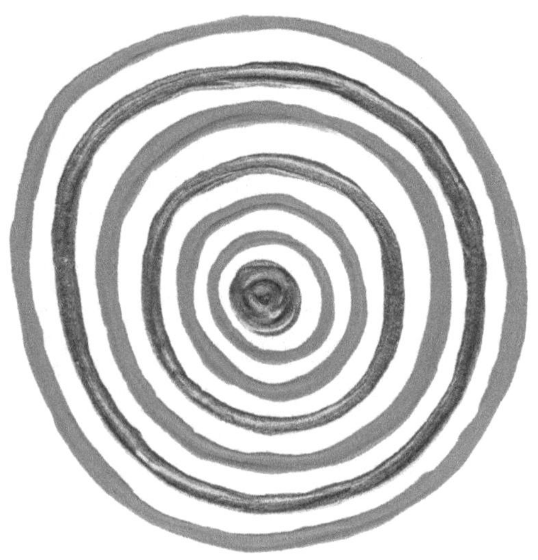

Brief description:

Gabriel stands for the development towards perfection at all levels. This circle works from the inside to the outside. The energy of this symbol spreads out in your body in a wave-like manner. What is happening now dissolves bit by bit, whatever helps you take the next step on your pathway to yourself!

For me the symbol of perfection is a valuable companion right from the beginning. If I find myself in a difficult stage of transformation or further advancement, I imagine that the symbol begins to shine in my solar plexus and like waves pulses outwards from the inside. Like the image of a drop falling into water, the waves spreading out, the rings becoming ever larger. And with every light and power wave I become more stable, and CALM and PEACE return to me.

Often I have simply just prayed in my own words, talked to Gabriel and prayed for divine order to be established within me.

Here in Power Ho'oponopono you implement it for harmony and PEACE.

3. The symbol of the Archangel Metatron:

To intensify your power of the heart.

Brief description:

Archangel Metatron provides the connection from the divine Heart to the divine source of your origin. The Divine Heart conveys basic trust and always helps you to come to yourself! The power and energy of Metatron resides in this sign. This force is always tailored to the individual on whom it works. Thus intensity of the symbols that you receive from me are adjusted to your own level of development. Before I do any energy work I connect with the divine Heart through this symbol and pray for a clear flow of information and energy.

The Metatron symbol accompanies me the whole day, but this will be different for different people. For me Metatron is very present, a kind of fatherly energy that guides, teaches and protects. He's been at my side since the beginning onwards, since my opening. Wise, teaching and protecting.

Here in Power Ho'oponopono it helps the power of your heart to open ever more and to recognize it.

4. The symbol of the Archangel Chamuel:

For unconditional Love.

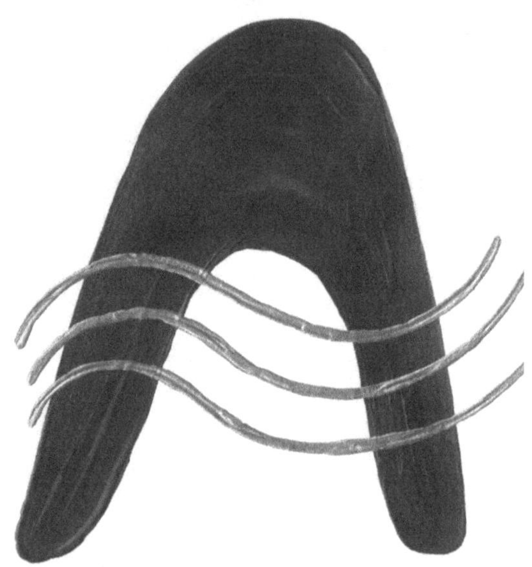

Brief description:

Development and intensification of neutrality and unconditional love.

Humility – to serve.

Humility is the courage to follow the word of God and to serve.

LOVE. The divine, unconditional love.

I love to use this symbol in working with children and for support in any of my work. It is also very helpful at whatever level, when bits of EGO become prominent. And in my view no-one is free from the ego. It's always there and always tries to push itself into the foreground. I've had to deal quite a lot with my own ego and through the love of Chamuel it becomes faster to identify and then easier to work with it.

Here in Power Ho'oponopono this symbol connects you with the solution, however it might become visible, namely always in LOVE!

Chapter 4

Activating and handling of the symbol energies

So how do you activate the Power Ho'oponopono principle and handle the energies of the symbols? Here is a simple guide to activating the four symbols:

Connect with trust and begin now.

Now make the clear decision to take all the steps that are intended for you and take full RESPONSIBILITY for EVERYTHING.

Take some time to be quiet for a moment in appreciation of yourself and for this work.

Prepare a room so that you feel relaxed in it.

Turn off all the phones and make yourself comfortable. Also with some music of your own choice, which feels harmonious to you for this particular occasion.

We'll now provide you with two variations for activation of the symbols. Both are equally effective. Choose for yourself the version that feels most harmonious to you.

First variation:

ACTIVATION by using BREATH.

Take the 4 symbols of the archangels between both hands and breathe 20 times in a "circle". That means you breathe the energy of angels through your left arm into your heart chakra, let the energy flow through your chest into the right arm, and from there through the right hand and return to the left hand and then start all over again.

This creates a breathing circuit!

In this way let the four angels flow through your heart! Twenty times!

Then, with the symbols in hand-please breathe 20 times deep into the abdomen and exhale, so that the abdominal wall rises on inhalation and again lowers when you exhale.

Second Variation:

ACTIVATION through LAYING on the heart chakra.

Prepare your room exactly as carefully as before. Select a melody that lies close to your heart, and take your time.

Now lay the four symbols on your heart chakra, close your eyes and ask the archangels to activate the energies of the symbols in your own energy system, to the degree of power and intensity best suited for your highest benefit. Stay relaxed with the symbols and observe what happens.

Once you've done that, the symbols activate in your energy system and in your heart. You can time this procedure according to your own needs. However, for the first activation, you should take at least 15 minutes, and longer is better.

After this first activation, it is no longer necessary to repeat this. But of course you can do it again and again when you have the impulse to do so.

At the beginning of each Power Ho'oponopono work: Lay the four symbols next to you, become quiet for a moment of silence and activate the energies. Take each symbol in your hand one-by-one, and imagine as you do so a green button ready to be activated. With each individual symbol imagine pressing the green button, asking the angels to be present in this work and imbue your actions with power and intensity, enough, so that the greatest good is achieved for all concerned.

As you do so, trust that everything happens very simply.

Clarity for beginners:

At the beginning of this work, I recommend you plan to take time and peace and calm to address Power Ho'oponopono. Initially, it is also very helpful to take each symbol individually in your own hands when speaking. Later on this isn't necessary. Once you are practiced you can apply the principle always and everywhere.

Then begin to say the following four sentences (along with your respective issue) loudly, softly or silently to yourself.

The basic concept of the Power Ho'oponopono principle includes the following words:

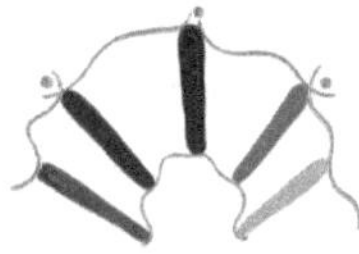

I accept complete responsibility for…

(Archangel Michael)

I am at peace with it.

(Archangel Gabriel)

I thank you in particular, all of you,
I thank life…

(Archangel Metatron)

I send LOVE. To me, to you, the situations that are to be healed!

(Archangel Chamuel)

Detailed examples are to be found on the following pages.

Chapter 5

Practical examples taken from life

Using examples, we will show you the process and bring it closer to you. We will describe the first example fully in words. With the others we will be briefer.

The important thing is the following:

Let yourself fall absolutely into the feeling of the situation, release the feelings and dive into the energies that appear. The more the heart energy can begin to work, the faster the change, healing or harmonizing can happen, both inner and outer. In the early days I sometimes worked for days at a time on some situations and feelings. Again and again and again I addressed the Power Ho'oponopono until I eventually noticed that NOW it really comes from the heart. From the very inside … now I can go in peace with everything that was. Believe me, even if you can't access this feeling right now, you will eventually feel it. You'll feel the difference when relief, liberation and the feeling of peace appear in the given situation.

First example:

The energy of fear

Fear can manifest itself very diversely and even unconsciously. I'd like to here also discuss the fear of doing the wrong thing. The fear to speak Ho'oponopono wrongly, to be afraid that it doesn't work if you don't hold exactly to our protocol.

Please believe me. It will work! It's very important that you speak it in the way that is coherent with yourself, based on our description.

Think of the Hawaiian family. Every family has given this principle its own individual touch. And think about the potato salad example. It works. TRUST IT.

So, back to the example of fear and its many facets.

- Fear of doing something wrong
- Fear of failure
- Fear of breaking down, collapsing
- Fear of sickness
- Fear of an accident
- Fear of something happening to your child
- Fear of going jogging or walking into the forest alone
- Fear of spiders or similar phobias
- Fear of one's own greatness
- Fear of showing yourself as you really are
- Existential angst
- Fear of heights
- Fear of commitment
- Fear of loss

And so on, and so on. Here, there are no limits set and usually it is very individual, and more intensely when you are dealing with your self.

1. Now take **the symbol of the Archangel Michael** in your hand or lay it on your heart chakra. (You can't do anything wrong here).

Then say aloud, softly, or to yourself in your thoughts the following words, and try to feel them:

"I accept full responsibility for my fear (for example), of doing something wrong, regardless of space or time, whenever this fear, this energy manifests in me; howsoever I have lived or still live this fear, in active or passive form".

(the formulation of "in active or passive form" will be explained at the end, on page ???).

Here I call upon the energy of fear as I feel it in me, or in whatever area of my life it is present and in which it constantly reappears!

For example:

Where do YOU have fear of doing something wrong?

- Fear, to behave falsely towards your partner?
- Fear, to choose the wrong words in a conversation important to you?
- Fear not to suffice as a woman, as a mother, as a lover, and to do something wrong in these areas?
- Fear to bring up your children wrongly?
- Fear of making a mistake while driving your car?
- Fear of making the wrong choices in your life?

I could carry on with this list forever. For you right now the task is to feel deeply within and be sincere with yourself. Where do you feel your issues? In which areas of your life do they occur? Every little feeling counts – because even the biggest avalanche starts with a small snowball.

And now ask Archangel Michael for the following:

"Archangel Michael, touch with your blue sword all links, entanglements and situations all the way back to my beginnings, and dissolve all that can and should be dissolved. Heal all that may and should be healed. Separate that which may and should be separated."

2. Now take **the symbol of the Archangel Gabriel** in your hand or lay it on your heart chakra and say the following:

   "I go in PEACE with myself, with the situation, and with all the feelings that I carry within myself. In peace, both within and without, with all the people who awaken or mirror in me the fear of doing the wrong thing, and for this purpose I ask you, Archangel Gabriel, to support the energy of peace in me."

   To this end, **utilize the following image:** imagine the seven circles of the symbol of Archangel Gabriel within you, radiating from inside to outside. Like a stone causes the water to ripple when you throw it in the water. Imagine these circles of peace in you spreading out, further and further.

3. Now take **the symbol of the Archangel Metatron** in your hand or lay it on your heart chakra and say:

"I thank all the people, souls, and energies, wherever and whenever they came into my life, which have shown me the energy of fear and/or have mirrored it, in active or passive form."

Here: if certain individuals occur to you, or appear in your thoughts – name them directly and send them your thanks.

"I thank you, X, for showing me this energy in me and making this experience available to me."

They are good teachers, even if in the first moment the experiences that arose from it, did not feel particularly pleasant. With the support of the symbol of the Archangel Metatron, now send them THANKS from your HEART. This is the energy to intensify the power of your heart.

4. Now take **the symbol of the Archangel Chamuel** in your hand or lay it on your heart chakra and say:

"With the help of the Archangel Chamuel I send LOVE, pure unconditional LOVE, to all these people, souls and to myself. I love myself and I love you all."

Unconditional love is healing.

Here you can imagine how the symbol – a big A – spans over the situation and the feelings at hand, allowing the energy of love to flow!

There are two possible closing sentences that we like to use:

"I will go in peace with myself, the others and the situations, as they are."

Or:

"THANK YOU, and so be it."

The significance of perpetrator and victim energies

Here is the explanation of how the meaning of perpetrator and victim energies in the course of the new age was transmitted to us. In the conventional world one always speaks of victims and perpetrators. We have taken a different approach for ourselves because this formulation was no longer authentic.

We now speak of actively or passively lived energies.

On our path we continually encounter the offender and victim roles. The idea is that we should dissolve these roles within us.

In the area of victim energy: self-sacrifice, allowing yourself to be used, exploited, to suffer, to bend over backwards, and so on.

In the area of offender energy: to abuse others, to impose your opinion or behavior on others and thus be actively disrespectful, or simply to use others for your own purposes.

We were also taught that we must dissolve both sides, sides we have often experienced in this and former lives. However, our perspective on this issue has now changed. Because consider: what if a soul consciously takes on a task to experience something and thereby takes on a role in which it is essential that a passive or active energy is created in order to really have that experience? And in that way heal the energies and issues contained in the experience.

When, for example, we don't feel or notice dependency, we don't have the possibility to heal it in ourselves. Thus, it is necessary that someone deliberately exploits (active) this dependency, which we live (passive). When, after this experience, we become conscious of this energy within us and are ready to change it, then we can harmonize, accept or heal these feelings and energies.

It is so important that both sides are available. Imagine, what would electricity be without a positive and negative polarity? It couldn't flow. Magnetism: without a north and south pole, there would be no polarity at all and the earth would come to a standstill. This means that these active and passive energies are essential and hence urgently belong to LIFE.

Again: it is right and natural that both sides are available. There is no "good" and no "bad". Both sides have their place. In this, trust your feelings, your inner voice and your intuition.

Second example:
The energy of deceit

Passive:
I was cheated on my partnership, in the financial or professional fields. By friends or family, as in, for example, inheritance.

Active:
I am the one who cheats, even when it is in minimal nuances. This energy knows no small or big, little or a lot.

The energy IS.

That means when I cheat the tax office by slipping in a few bills that don't actually belong in my return, then the energy of deceit accompanies it. The same with insurance and fraudulent liability claims, and so on. There are many areas in life that one can cover up with justifications, and many do this.

Here everyone must look at themselves and the more honest you are with yourself, the more you'll be able to begin to change your life.

1. Now take the **symbol of the Archangel Michael** in your hand or lay it on your heart chakra. Then say aloud, softly, or to yourself in thought the following words, and try to feel them as you say them:

   "I accept completely the responsibility for (for example) the betrayal of my partner, the fraud at the tax office, or generally for any energy of deceit within me. Independent of time or place, whenever these energies of deceit have manifested in me. However I have lived them or still live them, in active or passive form."

   And now ask Archangel Michael for the following:

   "Archangel Michael, touch with your blue sword all connections, entanglements and situations all the way back

to my beginnings, and dissolve all that can and should be dissolved. Heal all that may and should be healed. Separate that which may and should be separated."

2. Now take the **symbol of the Archangel Gabriel** in your hand or lay it on your heart chakra and say:

   "I go in PEACE with myself, with the situations and all the feelings that I carry within me. In peace within me and without with all the people who show me, or mirror within me, the energy of deceit, and I ask Archangel Gabriel to support the energy of peace within me."

3. Now take the **symbol of the Archangel Metatron** in your hand or lay it on your heart chakra and say:

   "I thank all the people, souls, and energies, wherever and whenever they came into my life, who have shown me or mirrored in me the energy of deceit, whether in active or passive form."

   Here: when you think of certain people, or they reveal themselves to you, or are in your thoughts, then name them directly and send them your thanks. They are good teachers, even if in the first moment the experiences which followed did not feel very pleasant. Now send THANKS from your HEART with the support from the symbol of Archangel Metatron. The energy for strengthening the power of your heart.

"I thank you, X, that you have shown me this energy and made available this experience."

4. Now take the **symbol of the Archangel Chamuel** in your hand or lay it on your heart chakra and say:

"With the help of Archangel Chamuel I send LOVE, pure unconditional love, to all these people, souls and myself. I love myself and I love all of you."

Closing sentences:

"I will go in peace with myself, the others and the situations, as they are."

Or:

"THANK YOU, and so be it."

Third example:

The energy of lies or denial

Passive:
I am being lied to in my partnership, in the financial or professional fields. By friends or family. Lies can appear in any mirror image of life. I myself am being abnegated or people or events in my life.

Active:
I am the one who lies, even when it is in small nuances. And as we already are aware, this energy knows no small or big, little or much. The energy IS.

The so-called necessary lies also carry this energy. This is the time to shine a light within, and everyone will find a part of themselves that is involved in lies or denial.

1. Now take the **symbol of the Archangel Michael** in your hand or lay it on your heart chakra. Then say aloud, softly, or to yourself in thought the following words, and try to feel them as you say them:

   "I accept complete responsibility for all the small 'necessary' lies to my parents, to avoid communicating my unease, or simply to have peace and quiet. I was also unauthentic to myself and my surroundings; and generally for any energy of the lie which is in

ME. Independent of time or place, whenever these energies of the lie have manifested in me. In whatever way I have lived them or still live them, in active or passive form."

Or use whatever specific lies, which now occur to you! Here you can check for yourself whatever lies have manifested themselves in your life in either active or passive form.

And now ask Archangel Michael for the following:

"Archangel Michael, touch with your blue sword all connections, entanglements and situations all the way back to my beginnings, and dissolve all that can and should be dissolved. Heal what can and should be healed. Separate that which may and should be separated."

2. Now take the **symbol of the Archangel Gabriel** in your hand or lay it on your heart chakra and say:

   "I go in PEACE with myself, with the situations and all the feelings that I carry within me. In peace within me and without with all the people who show me, or mirror within me, the energy of lying, and ask Archangel Gabriel to support the energy of peace within me."

3. Now take the **symbol of the Archangel Metatron** in your hand or lay it on your heart chakra and say:

"I thank all the people, souls, and energies, wherever and whenever they came into my life, who have shown me or mirrored in me the energy of lying, whether in active or passive form."

Here: when you think of certain people, or they reveal themselves to you, or are in your thoughts, then name them directly and send them your thanks. They are good teachers, even if at first the experiences that followed did not feel very pleasant. Therefore send THANKS from your HEART with the support from the symbol of Archangel Metatron. The energy for strengthening the power of your heart.

"I thank you, X, that you have shown me this energy and made available this experience."

4. Now take the **symbol of the Archangel Chamuel** in your hand or lay it on your heart chakra and say:

"With the help of Archangel Chamuel I send LOVE, pure unconditional love, to all these people, souls and myself. I love myself and I love all of you."

Closing sentences:

> ***"I will go in peace with myself, the others and the situation, as they are."***

Or:

> ***"THANK YOU, and so be it."***

There will be additional subtopics, or feelings, that show themselves, so please work through these thoroughly. It may well happen that you begin with the energy of lies, and that once inner peace has been reached with this theme, that further underlying themes reveal themselves. For example, you may encounter the fear of rejection, so you go through the whole process (sentences and symbols) with this theme until you reach dissolution and relief. Yes, this could well take several passes through the process. But don't let this deter you from this "work", it is worth it!

Fourth Example:
Sickness

But how do I deal with issues in which there is no active or passive side of the energy or of the issue revealing itself? For example, I'm sick, acutely or chronically, and wish to work on this issue with Power Ho'oponopono.

A first step is to accept the PRESENT SITUATION AS IT IS in ITS TOTALITY.

1. Now take the **symbol of the Archangel Michael** in your hand or lay it on your heart chakra. Then say the following:

   "I accept my sickness, my body, and everything that goes with it utterly and completely. I assume the full and total responsibility for the creation of my illness. Independent of time or place, whenever these disease energies have manifested in me. And I ask you, Archangel Michael, to please touch with your blue sword all connections, entanglements, people and situations all the way back to my beginnings, and in the here and now, and to dissolve all that can and should be dissolved. Heal what can and should be healed. Separate that which may and should be separated."

2. Now take the **symbol of the Archangel Gabriel** in your hand or lay it on your heart chakra and say the following:

   "I go in PEACE with myself, with the situations and all the feelings that I carry within me. In peace within me and without with all the people who show

me, or mirror within me, the energy of disease, and ask Archangel Gabriel to support the energy of peace and harmony within me."

3. Now take the **symbol of the Archangel Metatron** in your hand or lay it on your heart chakra and say:

   "I thank all the people, souls, and energies, wherever and whenever they came into my life, who have shown me or mirrored in me the energy of disease, which has caused this state within me. They have shown me my weak points. Please, Archangel Metatron, help me to send thanks from my heart, from a pure heart."

4. Now take the **symbol of the Archangel Chamuel** in your hand or lay it on your heart chakra and say:

   "I send LOVE, pure unconditional love! To myself and to all who are involved. I love myself and I love all of you. Please, Archangel Chamuel, support me."

   Closing sentences:

   "I will go in peace with myself and the situation, as it is."

Or:

"THANK YOU, and so be it."

Please do this work, these passages, until you sense the feeling of peace and relief set in. If, during the process you feel the urge to change the wording, then please go ahead. This is YOUR healing work, so create it in such a way that it feels right for you (I can only say: 'potato salad' – smile).

It may be that subsequently a sub-theme or feeling suddenly appears; in this case please work through it with Power Ho'oponopono. While doing this, should you come across an active or passive facet, simply speak as in the prior examples.

Fifth Example:

Diseases of a physical or mental nature involving children/grandchildren.

From experience it has been found that in this issue, almost without exception, every person (except perhaps those who don't have children) can feel the difference between heart and mind.

Passive:
I have sick people around me, my children are sick or have some kind of abnormality. ADHD, dyslexia, phobias, anger, aggression, are bullied, etc. One could enumerate these items indefinitely.

Active:
I have a disease or abnormality .... of whatever kind.

1. Now take the **symbol of the Archangel Michael** in your hand or lay it on your heart chakra. Then say aloud, softly, or to yourself in thought the following words, and try to feel them as you say them: if you have children bring them into your consciousness.

   "I accept in totality the responsibility for the disease that my child/grandchild carries within him/her; that they have *(here please name the sickness or abnormality they have, if you are aware of it.)* ***Independent of time or place, whenever these illness energies have manifested in me. Howsoever I have lived them or still live them, in active or passive form."***

   And now ask Archangel Michael for the following:

   "And I ask you, Archangel Michael, to touch with your blue sword all connections, entanglements, people and situations all the way back to my beginnings, and in the here and now, and to dissolve all that can and should be dissolved. Heal what can and should be healed. Separate that which may be and should be separated."

2. Now take the **symbol of the Archangel Gabriel** in your hand or lay it on your heart chakra and say the following:

   "I go in PEACE with myself, with the situation and all the feelings that I carry within me. In peace within me

and without with all the people who show me, or mirror within me, the energy of disease, and ask Archangel Gabriel to support within me the energy of peace and harmony. I send you, my child/grandchild peace."

3. Now take the **symbol of the Archangel Metatron** in your hand or lay it on your heart chakra and say:

   "I thank all the people, souls, and energies, wherever and whenever they came into my life, who have shown me and/or mirrored the energy of illness, whether in active or passive form. I thank you, my child/grandchild from the depths of my heart."

   Here: when you think of certain people, or they reveal themselves to you, or are in your thoughts, then name them directly and send them your thanks. They are good teachers, even if at first the experiences that followed did not feel very pleasant. Therefore send THANKS from your HEART with the support from the symbol of Archangel Metatron. The energy for strengthening the power of your heart.

   "I thank you, X, that you have shown me this energy and made available this experience."

4. Now take the **symbol of the Archangel Chamuel** in your hand or lay it on your heart chakra and say:

"I send with the help of Archangel Chamuel LOVE, pure unconditional love! To myself and to all people and souls. I love myself and I love all of you. I love you my child/grandchild"

Closing sentences:

"I will go in peace with myself and the situations, as they are."

Or:

"THANK YOU, and so be it."

Closing Words

We have walked a very special path, which opened up in 2006. A path leading far from normality and into a crazy or 're-moved' state. 'Re-moved' to another place in life, in dealing with the sensitivity that suddenly had appeared in our lives. Prior to this time we had nothing to do with spirituality and made a point of making a wide berth around every healer we came across. We don't want to tell our whole story here, as that is amply described in our book "*M.A.C.H.T. Nimm Dein Leben in Deine Hand*".

It is important for us to mention we have learned on this path to ALWAYS trust and follow our own impulses. ALWAYS, and to authentically live these impulses, even when for those around they weren't at all comprehensible. Often at first they were not for us either.

You certainly know for yourself such situations, in which it can take days, weeks, or even months before this insight comes: "Ah, now I know what that was all about!"

We didn't understand much at first, but on the other hand how much can actually be understood on the level of the mind?

That was all a very intense and crazy time, but we wouldn't have missed a moment of it, because the feelings and experiences that arose from it have bestowed and enabled all these NEW INSIGHTS.

Illustrations of the four archangels symbols

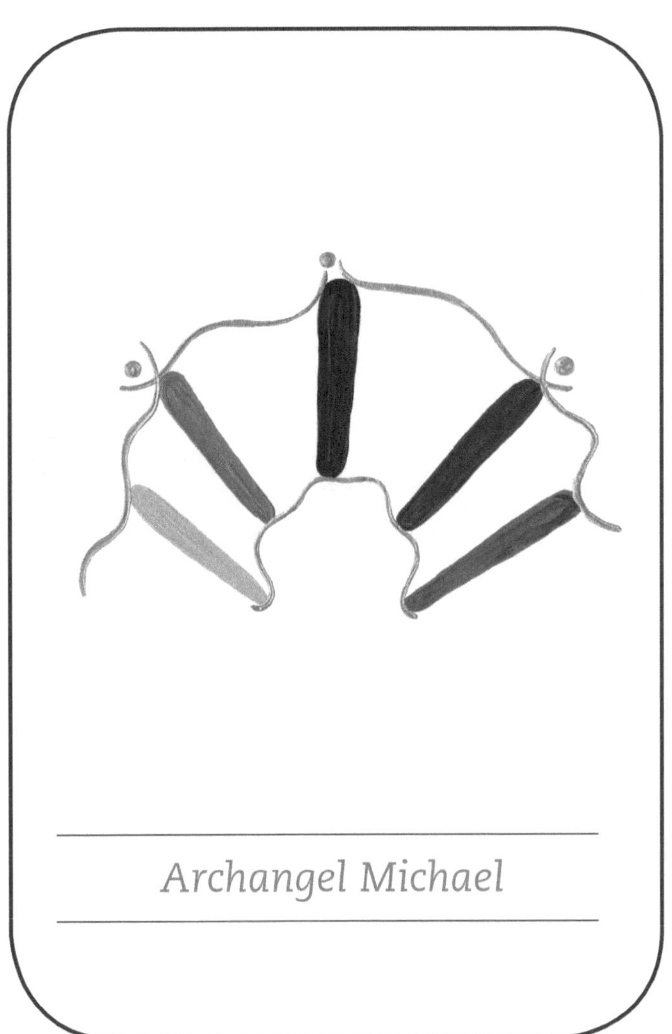
Archangel Michael

Archangel Gabriel

Archangel Metatron

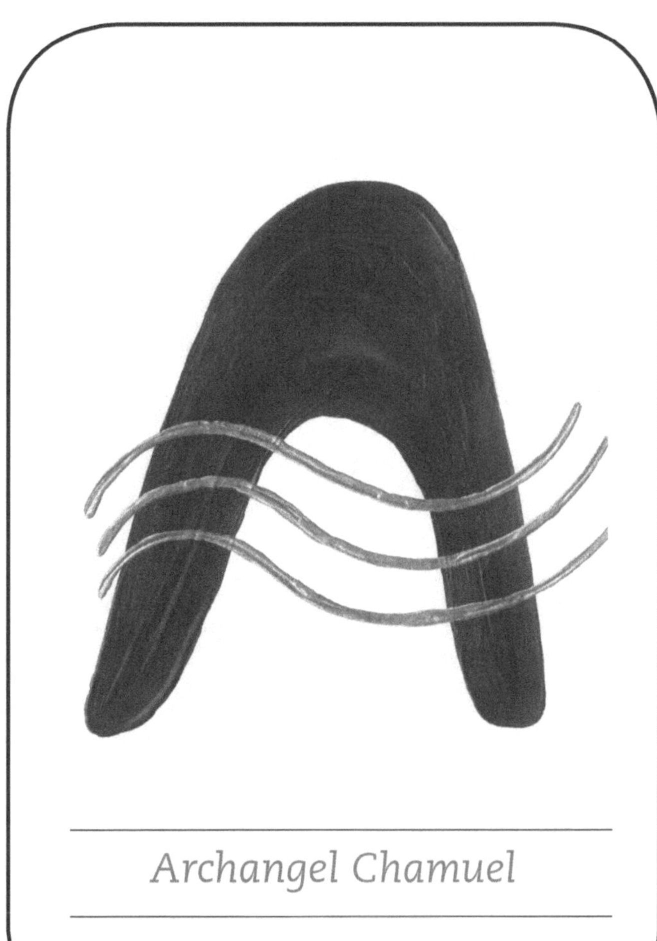
Archangel Chamuel

Bibliography

Vitale, Joe and Len, Ihaleakala Hew:
Zero Limits – The Secret Hawaiian System for Wealth, Health, Peace & More.
John Wiley & Sons, Inc., Hoboken, New Jersey, 2007

Salopek, Christine und Robert:
M.A.C.H.T *Nimm Dein Leben in Deine Hand.*
tao.de in J. Kamphausen Verlag und Distribution GmbH, Bielefeld, 2012

Institute of HeartMath©
www.heartmath.org

FineArt prints of Energy Images on canvas

FineArt art prints on high quality canvas stretched on frames

Light resistant UV printing, frames made of natural wood

Personally signed and prepared with the energy of Christine Salopek

Various sizes and designs possible

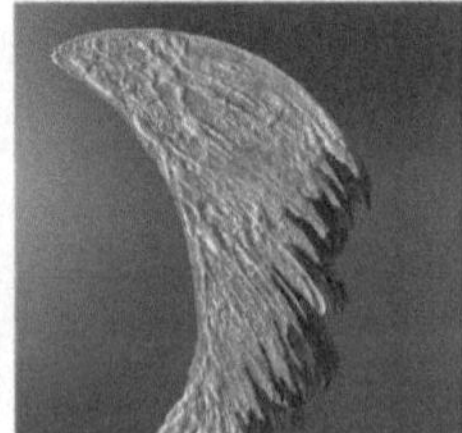

Meditation CDs

Joy Meditation (CD)
Guided meditation by Christine Salopek
Price: 15 Euros

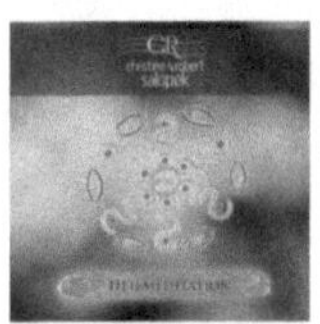

Healing Meditation (CD)
Guided meditation by Christine Salopek
Price: 15 Euros

Energy Raising Meditation (CD)
Guided meditation by Christine Salopek
Price: 15 Euros

Heart Meditation (CD)
Guided meditation by Christine Salopek
Price: 15 Euros

Chakra Meditation (2 CDs)
Guided meditation by Christine Salopek
Price: 24.90 Euros

More from Christine & Robert Salpek

See online shop at

www.spirit-solution.com

and

www.christine-salopek.de

www.justwomen.de

www.authentic-academy.de

www.silenos.de

spiritsolution
SILENOS®
GESICHTS- UND KÖRPERCREME
AUTHENTIC
ACADEMY
spirit
EoSoS
solar
AUTHENTIC
LIFE COACH®
just
WOMEN®
by christine salopek
CR
christine & robert
salopek

Zeitfracht Medien GmbH
Ferdinand-Jühlke-Straße 7
99095 Erfurt, Deutschland
produktsicherheit@kolibri360.de